Desert Trails

June A. Reynolds

Desert Trails

ReadersMagnet, LLC

Desert Trails
Copyright © 2020 by June A. Reynolds

Published in the United States of America
ISBN Paperback: 978-1-951775-72-8
ISBN eBook: 978-1-949981-05-6

All rights reserved. No part of this publication may be reproduced, stored in a retrieval system or transmitted in any way by any means, electronic, mechanical, photocopy, recording or otherwise without the prior permission of the author except as provided by USA copyright law.

The opinions expressed by the author are not necessarily those of ReadersMagnet, LLC.

ReadersMagnet, LLC
10620 Treena Street, Suite 230 | San Diego, California, 92131 USA
1.619.354.2643 | www.readersmagnet.com

Book design copyright © 2020 by ReadersMagnet, LLC. All rights reserved.
Cover design by Ericka Obando
Interior design by Shemaryl Tampus

Contents

Baboquivari 8
   A Nation unto Itself 8
Measure the Mountain 11
Baboquivari Campground 12
Waw Gi Wulk 13
At Home on the Range:
(Near Tonto National Monument)
Following the Cow Trails 14
The Chicken Feeding Song 17

The Story of Gold Flower Road 19
   At the Prospector Trail 19
   Franny 20
   Jennifer 21
   Pete Saves the Day 27
   Stolen Goods Returned 29
   Dad Was Right 30
   Reporting the Dress 33
   Pete Finds Out the Mystery 34
   Jennifer Warns Franny 35
   All that is Silver is not Gold 36

Just off the Yetman Trail	38
He-Who-Sits	41
Gwenny Ruth	43
Delano St. Tucson, AZ	43
Stairway to the Clouds	47
The Hugh Norris Trail	47
Juan Carlos Trail	54
Buffalo Soldier	55
Your Broad Face	56
The Naturalist Hiker: (An Essay) On the Utah/Arizona Border	58
Like Rocks	58
The Magic Stones	59
Hike up Aravaipa Canyon	61
The Bar at the End of the Trail…	62
The Dutchman Trail On Superstition Mountain	62
Iron Ranger Song at Picket-Post Trail	67
The Bar at the End of the Trail: Part 2	69
Hiking Terms	72
Virga	76

Baboquivari

A Nation unto Itself

The Tohono O'odham of Southwest Arizona

In the Sonoran Desert people of this place are known as the "desert people." Their country encompasses a land the size of Connecticut and is ringed by massive mountain ranges on the north and west sides. To the south, runs the Mexican border. From far away, most of the people can see Baboquivari, a high point of rock in which the people believe the creator, I'itoi lives. Indeed, the desert wilderness foothills up against the Baboquivari Mountain range is very special and holy. The people come at various times of the year to worship, harvest the saguaro cactus, and connect with each other. We are honored to camp on this place each year. Among the range beasts (beef cows) ranched by the natives, there is a diverse number of animals, insects, plants, and birds.

Since 1694, when Father Kino found these people, the Tohono O'odham have been hunter/gatherers of the desert. They speak a Pima language much like their northern neighbors and cousins, the Papago. They have much in common with their neighbors, despite the mountains in between them. In the early days, these people lived on mesquite beans, saguaro cactus fruits, and ground desert seeds. Game such as deer and javelins rounded out their diet. The people ranged widely over the desert at various times of year to take advantage of prized food and other needs. The people were known to go as far as the Baja California area for forage as well as to go north to visit and trade with others.

Even though the people live on a border, they traditionally have an extended territory and are related not only to the people on Mexican side of the land but also to the land itself. There are some of the Tohono O'odam people who have title to land on the other side of the border and they farm in those areas.

In the 21st century, these people are good stewards of their land and reflect the wider culture of the state of

Arizona. They look upward for the clouds which get hooked on the mountains for precious rain. They look hopefully forward in spite of climate change. They find themselves in the middle of political winds from Latino migrants and border patrol officials. They remain true human beings.

Measure the Mountain

Let me measure every member of your spires—every crevice of your skin. Seeking shadows of rock outcropping—imaginatively shelter what might have been.

Witness fishbone ridges light on fire, with the sinking of the sun. Behold boulders, newly fired—birth of MOON and the HUMAN.

Baboquivari Campground

We are honored that the Tohono O'odham people allow us to camp at the base of Babaquivari, their sacred mountains and the "Center of the Universe." Truly, every year that we come there, something unexpected and very magical happens.

Here, the bare ground is filled with dark red, fine ground granite. The grains are a combination of quartz, feldspar, hematite, rhyolite, and iron, giving the ground a dark-brown color.

In the parking area and fair grounds of the Tohono O'odham natives there are footprints—many months of signatures of the people. Today, as I make my statement on the ground, the sun glowingly revealed the little prints of a child in tennis shoes. Then I see that sometimes there are identical prints, only larger beside the small ones. Other times I see the small prints stop next to a dual-wheel truck tire print.

Suddenly, the prints are not so flat footed. Rushing, the feet point to a small sloping trail, down to a camp area. Down to where the elders sit on benches under the oak trees; ready to tell stories or sing a song.

Waw Gi Wulk

Sitting where the elders sat,
Their eyes cast up at Waw Gi Wulk.
The green glow of afternoon, looks upon tumbled rocks
below,
like the chaos of mankind.

From up on top, he looks north and south.
He looks upon us across the windy valleys,
And sighs.

12/09/15

At Home on the Range

(Near Tonto National Monument)

Following the Cow Trails.....

A dusky peach light slowly envelops the night sky and the orange spotlight sun hikes its way over the twin peaks. Sentinel Cow climbs the ridge on this morning from her warm, soft bed in the sand from the wash. She looks back on her growing twins, still snoozing on the ground. She is the lead cow on the range in these parts, but she is not the only one in the sixty-square-mile land.

Slowly, she picks her way up the slope, around the cactus and yuccas. Finally she reaches the top and smells the breeze. She stands one way and looks down. She stands the other way and looks up. She quickly gazes at the water about twenty miles below. It was a nice summer down

there. Now it is turning to fall. The breeze is not warm, it is cold.

She sees a handful of her kind on one side of the hill so she follows the ridge to be in line with them. There, in a fold of the land, she finds a tender Palo Verde with branches that the deer have missed. She hungrily bites them off with a mighty snap. The next branch is higher and she cranes her neck up to the sky. She wraps her tongue around the branch and…snap. It is off, and she is munching the sweet juicy leaves. Then she nibbles daintily on the other side.

Crunch, crunch, crunch. Suddenly, out of the corner of her eye she sees movement. She turns both eyes at the movement and sound and stares head-on. She sees two hikers. They are coming over the opposite ridge. She normally sees hikers on the hiking trails or roads. They are never this high on the hill by the water truck. Only one has a stick, but she is not holding it like a gun. They are not hunters—they are hikers The two are walking on the ridge and one is wearing a flappy hat that is blowing in the cool breeze.

"Mooooooo!" She sounds the alarm. She moves away from her succulent tree and plows down the ridge. The young calves and their mothers scatter. They know something is happening. Some see the hikers and stare. The young ones dance around this way and that, flinging their heads around and kicking their hind legs like bucking broncos.

Sentinel Cow watches. She now sees there is no danger. The hikers keep hiking through on their ridge, glancing over and taking a few pictures. The little calves are racing down the hill and into the wash. She feels that they are such foolish creatures. She does her duty as she marches between the calves and the hikers, trying to marshal some order.

The Chicken Feeding Song

Oh, come a' runnen'
come a' runnen'
come a' runnen'
Oh, come a' runnen' to me.

Oh, come a' runnen'
come a' runnen'
come a' runnen'
Oh, come a' runnen' to me.

I've got gold in my pocket, in my pocket
Oh, come a' runnen' to me.

I've got silver in my saddle, in my saddle.
Oh, come a' runnen' to me.

I've got lead in my shot gun, yes my shot gun.
Oh, come a' runnen' to me.

I've got turkey in my oven, in my oven
Oh, come a' runnen' to me.

The Story of Gold Flower Road

At the Prospector Trail

Every morning after the first rooster crow and just as the sun came over the twin peak's range, Franny Aiken would be out there among the dead lawnmowers, barrels, cracked toilets, and tires, feeding her chickens and assorted ducks and wild turkeys. She came to live on Gold Flower Road as soon as the bulldozer went through the desert and carved a dirt road. Her husband was a hired hand at the Double Bar X Ranch. When he died in 1980, Rex Armstrong, the ranch owner, set Franny up in a used 1970 mobile home, right there in the new wildcat subdivision.

It wasn't anything fancy, just a dusty old dirt road and an acre lot, but she could raise a pig if she wanted to. Franny did have a little fuzzy burro, Percy, which turned out to be her pride and joy.

Franny

The morning of the accident was all a' glory. We had monsoon rains for two days. So when the clouds cleared out and the sun popped over the mountain range, I knew that I would not be cooped up in the mobile home, knitting sweaters and hats for people who had too many already. I ran out to the backyard and got Percy all ready to go with two matching ore bags and several shovels, picks, and water. We were off to the foothill mines. The mines were closed in the late 1950s and the Bureau of Land Management were in charge of the land. Some of the mines had not been filled in or fenced, so we would sneak up there early so's nobody would see us. There is also supposed to be no camping, but it is the 1990s and lots of Mexicans are crossing the border to get jobs. Some go as far north as Washington State. They have camps on the lower ridges where no one can see them, but from the mines, I can see them. They don't stay more than a few days.

Well, I should'a been more careful because the rocks were washed by the rains and so they are rolly polly or so loose you can start an entire avalanche. That's what happened. I got into the mine hole and slid twenty feet, right into a big lake of water. I  tried to work my way up on three sides and every time, I slid right down into the bottom. I stumble on a rock on the way up out of the mine and rolled down again. That is when I think I broke my arm, looking back at it. Percy got a little antsy after about four hours and started braying. This got the Mexicans down in the lower foothills running up the hill to see what was going on. One of them went down to my neighbor's house to get help. Then the Mexicans all packed up and started walking into town so the Drexel Fire Department would not see them. I was so upset about the accident that it wasn't until I got out that I realized that I had broken my arm.

Jennifer

Hi. My name is Jennifer. I moved in with Great Aunt Franny after the mine accident. I was a sophomore at the High School and my Mom ran away with some, as my Dad says, "male floosie" to Wyoming. My mom had no interest in me and I didn't give a rip about her, but my Dad was a sweetheart. He was a welder for the Titan missiles, but he got laid off with the end of the Cold War. He decided that he would go to Alaska for a year and work on the oil pipeline. I could stay with Franny and help her, since she had a broken arm. My Dad left an old Dodge Dart for me to drive and I got my license so I could go buy groceries. My other chore was to take care of Percy, the Burro. That meant watering and feeding him and moving his picket around in the yard. He also had stones stuck in his hooves from time to time, which I had to take out with a tool.

Aunt Franny's house was all decorated like the 1970s: Dark paneling, avocado-colored appliances, orange and shocking green curtains with those little Mexican balls hanging off of them, and a dark-brown shag rug.

One day I spoke up. "Aunt Franny, this place is so dark, it is like a cave. It looks like a hippie's den put together by Scooby Doo cartoon characters."

She laughed. "This is not a hippie's den, Jennifer. It's more like a house the Hippies inherited from their parents!"

"Well, that might be right, but it is 1995," I agreed. Maybe we could at least change the bathroom to a more updated pastel garden to at least make it look bigger." So we did manage to redecorate the bathroom and then we found out that we needed new things for the bathroom.

Going to a Goodwill store or any used-goods store is now called "thrifting."

All the stores are called "thrifts" as in a noun, and "thrifting" is a verb. I totally learn a lot about words in my English class. So early one Saturday, we went "thrifting." I carefully drove down Bopp, crossed over to Kinney, and then onto Gates Pass Road, which is a narrow, winding, high mountain pass into Tucson. I normally don't go into town much because our grocery store and my high school are on the south side of town and so I usually go there on the Ajo Highway. So here we were winding through the rocks, barely two lanes wide. Suddenly, there was a huge truck coming the other way.

"Oh Be-Jesus!" wheezed Franny. "For years, I usually take the bus from the south side and now I know why. I haven't been through this pass since it was a gravel road and mules carried heavy loads of rock."

Suddenly, around another curve, fifteen people on road bikes were ahead of us. I stomped on the brakes and watched the car tailgating me come very close to the back bumper. Our trip turned into slow motion for about a mile and then the car in back of me reared up and passed me and all the bikers. The car missed a tour bus coming the other way by about five feet!

We got on Speedway (which is a road that becomes a street through town) and passed the high-rise buildings of downtown. Then we started seeing the thrift stores. I found two sets of school clothes after hitting three stores. Franny was looking for bathroom items such as bathmats, towels, washcloths, and curtains. She was having lots of fun trying to match the colors with her wallpaper swatch. She saw a beautiful copper tea kettle and reached out for it. Then she pulled her hand away.

"Go ahead and buy it!" I prodded. Her old copper pot looked like is should have been in some museum.

"But it costs five dollars and I've already got a copper tea kettle," she said.

"It might inspire an update of the kitchen, if we get it," I observed.

"Well, you might be right," she said as she grabbed the teapot. "The old one is starting to leak."

This went on all day as we hit stores like the Iron Buffalo, the Good Find Store, and the Humane Society Store. We almost forgot about lunch so it was a late lunch at the Howling Jalapeno. The sun was just setting as we squeezed through the Golden Gate Pass once again.

Then tragedy struck. As we drove into our place we saw that the light we left on was barely hanging from a wire and was out. Luckily, I had a flashlight and I approached the porch. Both of the doors on the porch had been ripped off the hinges and were flapping in the breeze.

"What on earth happened?" yelled Franny as we entered the place. "Did we have a twister come through?"

But it was not a force of nature. It was man-made. The electric wires were ripped out of the main part of the outside of the house and there was no electricity. From the looks of the inside of the house, it looked like a whirlwind. Stuff was ripped off walls and every drawer in the house was opened and gone through. Some of the stuff was just laying all over the floor. I ran to my room. My CD player, CDs, and my watch were missing.

Aunt Franny's coin collection, china plates from her wedding, several small appliances, and even her old copper tea kettle was gone.

"Good thing I got a new tea kettle," said Franny bitterly as she lit the gas stove to put on some tea to steady her nerves.

I realized that these people were looking for anything made of metal and small items which could be pawned easily. I went back to my room and held my breath—there was a big hole in my closet. My prom dress that my Dad bought for me was missing. He bought it when we were in Phoenix when he went to his job interview.

My Dad looked at the brightly colored sequined dress that looked like a ball gown and said, "Sweetheart, I'm going to be gone for two years and I know that you are so beautiful that someone is going to ask you to the prom, so I'm going to get this for you."

It cost one-hundred and fifty dollars. It was a custom-made dress from Mexico. Now it is gone. It still had the price tag on it. I started to cry as I ran blindly to the neighbor's to call the sheriff. We sat waiting in the dark for him to come all night, but he didn't show up until the next day.

"So what do you got miss'en?" he said.

"Here is a list of what we have not found so far." I said shoving a two-page stapled list into his hands.

He whistled. "This is mighty impressive. You know these home invasions are becoming more common with all the tweakers and people with foreclosures. This economy has been too good for my business." He smiled as if he had told a joke.

Franny was quite grave. "This home invasion stuff is not new sir. Ever since this state was settled, marauding thieves raped and pillaged many a ranch house long before your cul-de-sac."

"Did they take any gold or silver? I mean now, not back then..." asked the sheriff with notebook and pen poised.

"Yep." Said Franny. They took my coin collection with three lead quarters from World War II and one gold Civil War coin that belonged to my great-grandfather.

"Oh," said the Sheriff as he wrote it down. "That's it?"

"That's it," said Franny.

"What about your neighbors?" asked the Sheriff. "Did they see anything?"

"The people across the street are deer hunting. The neighbors on either side work on Saturday." I said.

"Okay, that's it. I might ask around. I'll check all the pawn shops and see what's up." Then he got in his car and drove away.

Weeks passed and the days were pretty routine. Magically, we had an electrician working at our place and he was pretty busy rewiring the mobile home for a couple of days. Those darn copper robbers! Just how much money do they make selling electrical wiring?

It was great having lights again and a working refrigerator, but there was no radio, CD player, TV, or toaster to use the electricity. I noticed that even though I spent many hours picking up rocks in the yard, Percy had stones in his hooves just about every other day. Where did he pick up all those rocks?

I've gone to school with the same kids since first grade. They are a pretty rough bunch, but I'm pretty used to them. But after I moved in with Great Aunt Franny, they became well, a bit snarky. They always had some snide remark to make towards me that I did not understand. My math buddy, Pete, heard this girl named Ginger and her older brother, Joe, harassing me one day.

"Hey, Jennifer," said Ginger. "I heard you got robbed. Did they get everything?"

"Uh, yeah. How did you hear about it?" I asked.

"Oh it's all over TV and the radio," said Ginger.

"Yeah," said Joe. "You totally got wiped out. Didn't you see it?"

"How can I, Joe, since I don't have a TV or radio." I said.

"Oh that's too bad," mocked Ginger. "Why is it when you get on the news, you never get to see it?"

Pete cleared his throat. "Well I think that is the least of Jennifer's problems. Right now we have to study for a math test."

"Did they get everything?" asked Joe.

"Goodbye," I said as I walked away.

Pete Saves the Day

I started taking the bus to school to save on gas money. I thought that maybe I could save for at least a CD player. One Friday as I was working in the computer lab, the bell rang quite unexpectedly.

"What's that for?" I asked the librarian.

"It's the end of the day. We have a half day for teacher training," she said as she put on her sweater and got out her key. "I have to drive across town for my meeting."

Somehow I never got this memo. So I scooped up my stuff and headed out to the bus area. There were no buses. Everyone was getting into cars. Pete pulled up in front of me.

"Do you need a ride home?" he asked as he leaned out the window.

I was relieved. "Yes! Thank you Pete, thank you so much! I forgot about this half day thing," I said, sort of embarrassed.

"No problem." He said as he cleared off a place on the seat of his old, dusty Toyota truck.

The truck roared out of the parking lot and a group of kids with Ginger and Joe among them flipped us off.

"What the heck?" I said and looked at Pete.

Pete turned red under his white cowboy hat. "Uh well, I finally heard a rumor from that gang. They think that your

Great Aunt is holding out on everyone. They think that she is stink'en rich."

I laughed hysterically. "You have got to be kidding me. Someone actually believed that nonsense and that is why we got robbed?"

"I guess so." Said Pete.

"Well if she is so rich, why doesn't she go down to Cucrao and buy a TV, radio, toaster, CD player and..." I wanted to say prom dress, but I didn't.

We didn't say another word until we got to Bopp Road.

"Oh we should'a gone to the McDonalds for lunch." Said Pete.

"That's OK." I said. "If you've got time, I'll make you a real hamburger from fresh ground beef from the Double Bar X Ranch. Aunt Franny gets all her beef from them."

"Speaking of which, isn't that your Aunt Franny walking down the road?" asked Pete in surprise.

Sure enough there was Aunt Franny and Percy walking along the edge of Bopp Road. "So that's how that burro gets those rocks!" I burst out.

We slowly rolled to a stop in front of them and got out of the truck. She was as surprised to see us as we were her.

"Jennifer," she said. "Why aren't you in school? And who is this?" she said as she pointed Percy's harness at Pete.

"I forgot that there was a half day today only for the high school and that the buses were not going to run until 2:15. Pete is giving me a ride. But what are YOU doing out here on Bopp Road?"

She was going to lie, I could tell because she was going to scratch her ear. "Oh I just had to go to White's Hardware for a few things," she patted Percy's canvas bag and it looked to me like it was full of rocks.

"Well, let's give you a ride," said Pete as a car went whizzing by too fast on the road. He quickly opened his tailgate, pulled out two large, wide boards and said: "After you m'lady."

"Oh I couldn't possibly," said Franny.

"You can't get Percy in your truck," I said to Pete.

"Nonsense," said Pete. "I've hauled several calves and yearlings in this truck and even three AWOL goats all at once. Allow me."

He carefully took the reins, whispered something in Percy's ear, and he lead that animal right into the truck. He helped Franny get in and gave her a cooler to sit on. We got back in the truck and took off down the road at a slow, but steady pace. Pete and I stole glances at each other on the way to Gold Flower, but we didn't say a thing. While Pete and Franny got Percy out of the truck and back on his tether, I cooked up a big batch of burgers.

"Oh man, Jennifer! These burgers are the best!" exclaimed Pete.

"We get ground beef and sirloin from the ranch, every time a steer breaks a leg on the range," explained Franny.

I just rolled my eyes and went with the punches.

Stolen Goods Returned

The temperate winter was all but over. It was April, barbecue weather and everyone's favorite holiday of Arizona, Easter. The Papago Nation was blasting dynamite on a Friday night of the big holiday. We were in the middle of making some dinner, when the Sheriff rolled up to the mobile home. He had a big, orange cardboard box when he knocked at the door.

"Uh, hello, ma'am," coughed the Sheriff. "We have recovered some of your stuff. Sorry if there's black stuff on it. We dusted for fingerprints."

Franny pulled up a plastic chair on the two by four porch. "Thank you, sir, please sit down." She pulled up a chair too and I sat on the step below. There was the toaster, the CD player, a handful of old china dishes, vases, and silverware. Half of the coin collection was there; the three lead coins and some of the fifty state quarters.

"Oh, but no Civil War coin…" sighed Franny.

"Well since we recovered half of the collection, it could be that the robber or robbers still have what they thought was the better half of the collection," said the Sheriff with authority.

"Did you think that up yourself?" asked Franny, quite innocently.

"No. It's just more of the jibber jabber of the investigator of this case," he said in disgust.

Franny stood up. "Well, sir, Jennifer and I thank you so much for returning our things. Does this mean the case is closed?"

The Sheriff stood up. "Oh no, this case is not closed."

Dad Was Right

Much to my amazement, Pete asked me to the Prom. My dad was right for once. Franny and I went thrifting again and I found a nice dress that I thought would take the least amount of remodeling. My home economics teacher called the color of the dress "vintage white." We cut down the neckline and matched similar material to make the dress longer. It matched so well, you could not even see that it was different material. There was a huge baby-blue satin bow surrounding the waist and the same satin was used to cap the neckline and short sleeves on the seams of the dress. It made the dress "stand up and stand out" according to my teacher.

Pete came to pick me up in his father's white tub of an Oldsmobile a half an hour late. He had all his prom clothes on when a couple of calves jumped a fence to get back to their mothers. No one else was home, so Pete took off all his prom clothes, put on his work clothes caught the calves, and got dressed again.

"I almost forgot my new hat." He said as he tipped it for me and held open the car door. He had on his best boots, new black pants, white shirt, bolo tie, and a black leather vest. The hat, of course was white, but was a felted Stetson which probably cost more than my prom dress.

Just before the announcement of the prom queen, there was a disturbance in the hallway of the gym. It was so loud that even the live band stopped playing and stood there looking at the hallway. There was the junior class advisors, Ms. Pine and Mr. Longbow arguing with two guys and a younger girl.

Mr. Longbow, a Native American, was a big guy. He was really leaning in on one of the guys. He grabbed his shirt front and tie and walked him out the door. There was lots of argument as to whether he was drunk or not. The other two kids came walking in. It was Ginger and Joe and…

I sucked in some air and whispered. "My God! My God! Ginger is wearing my prom dress!" I was trembling and Pete quietly led me to a dark corner table.

"The one that got stolen?" he asked.

"Yes." I said.

"Could it possibly be that she bought a dress just like yours?"

"Well, maybe but...my Dad bought it in Phoenix way last spring." I said. "It was a custom-made dress from Mexico. I didn't see any others like it."

Pete trained his eyes on Ginger as she trotted around the room giggling and chatting with all the younger girls. "That dress doesn't look like it fits her very well. It looks like she's about to bust out of it and, well it looks kind of long. Yeah she's stepping on the hem."

I felt a headache coming on. "What are we going to do, Pete?

Before he could answer, everyone was focused on the stage. It was time for the crowning of the queen. Ms. Pine held the crown over all the princesses heads dramatically and finally she clamped the crown on Annabelle Armitage—the smartest, although not the prettiest girl on the court. Everyone cheered, except for Ginger.

"Boo! Boo!" she screamed. "Selena Branchton should'da got it!" She started stamping her feet.

Quickly, Ms. Pine directed all the court members off the stage and Annabelle and her escort got ready to do the queen's dance. Ms. Pine urged the band to start playing the slow song. At the same time Mr. Longbow raced over to Ginger and escorted her out of the gym. Ginger's brother just sat and watched.

Pete got up and got us some punch and cookies. Pete drank some of the punch and spit it out on the wall of the gym.

"Don't drink that, Jennifer, it's spiked!" Pete was going to get up and tell Mr. Longbow, but he must have been alerted, because across the room Mr. Longbow was hauling off the punchbowl. Joe left. The entertainment was over for him. The rest of the evening, we danced the fast dances until we were sweaty then we got some air by the door and then danced a few slow dances before the end.

Reporting the Dress

The next day, I called the Sheriff, but it was Sunday, so he didn't get back to me on the phone until late Monday afternoon. He came out to the place Tuesday after school.

"So, little lady," he said as he overburdened the plastic chair on the porch, "What makes you think you know who the robbers are?"

"Well, I have some evidence." I said. "This girl, Ginger Hill in my class was wearing my prom dress at the prom. I am pretty sure that it was the dress. It is one of a kind, purchased in another town, and it didn't fit Ginger right."

The Sheriff chuckled. "The old Cinderella complex, eh?"

I got hot. "I don't find it funny, sir. It was an expensive gift from my father who I won't see for another year. It was a special dress made in Mexico."

"I can't get a warrant with that," he sighed.

I tried to be calm. "Well, there was a tag in the hem of the dress that said: 'Hencho de Amour de Angelisso'—will that help?"

The Sheriff pulled out his notebook and wrote it down. "Now you might have something there. If the dress shop can verify that there were specific seamstresses who sewed labels into the dresses, we might have grounds to investigate closer. That will give our bloodhound investigator something to do. Let me see if there is anything we can do. Is that everything?"

"Yes." I said. I kept thinking, *why does everyone always ask that question? It is as if we are hiding something that they already know about.*

Pete Finds Out the Mystery

A few weeks after the prom, I finally found out the gossip that had been going around the country for so long about Franny. I found out in the locker room after school as we were suiting up for baseball practice. The truth always comes out in the boy's locker room.

"It's like El Dorado." Said Max, the first baseman. "This old biddy has a burro and she goes gold mining up in the hills."

"Really? Said the catcher, "I thought you couldn't mine up there in the Tucson Mountains anymore."

"Yeah, but what's to stop her?" Said Max. "She can just say she is hiking and there is no ranger or anything out there to stop her."

"Hey Pete, don't you date her daughter, Jennifer?" said the catcher.

I shook my head. "That's not her daughter—are you crazy?—That's her great-niece."

"Well, whatever." Said Max. "Have you seen any gold stashed around?"

I shook his head again. "Not a fleck of gold."

Max stood up. "Well there's lots of guys out there talking about looking for the old lady's gold. They've got guns and they like to tear places apart. I'd be careful if I was you."

The catcher gathered up all his gear. "Those Hill kids are always yacking about that kind of stuff. I am so sick of them all the time. I'll be glad to graduate and get out of here."

"Well thanks, guys." I said nonchalantly as they walked away.

I told all this news to Jennifer and all she could say was "I knew it! I knew it."

Jennifer Warns Franny

I asked Franny about the gold mining and she admitted that she was doing it, all along. She also said she was looking for other minerals too, like copper and silver.

"AND, and so…" I said, trying to get some sort of admission.

"Well, it's just a hobby. I work on an easy mine now. No more pits or far-away places. In fact, the place I've been working on was my old friend Jim's claim."

"What does Jim think about you working his claim?" I asked.

"He doesn't think anything about it. He's dead," she said. "Look how do you think that I paid for the mobile home to be rewired? I cashed in all the ore I had, so I don't have any more."

I folded my arms. "Well you need to get the news out there somehow because there are a lot of creeps out there who want to tear your house apart again and get your gold," I warned.

"That is advice well taken," said Franny.

All that is Silver is not Gold

A week after school was out, the temperature hit 103 and I was melting in the mobile home with Franny. The good news was that starting next week, I could take the bus on Bopp Road to the Mission Library and work at the air conditioned library.

Suddenly, a cloud of dust rolled into our driveway with the Sheriff. He jumped out of his car and said "We proved it, Jennifer! The dress is really yours and we found the gold Civil War coin at the Hill's residence. We've got at least two suspects in jail and I think there were more."

"So where's our stuff?" asked Franny.

"Oh it is evidence for now." There will be a trial in about three months, so you will get your dress back, Missy, by the next prom!"

I just looked at him and rolled my eyes.

Franny spoke up. "Well, thanks, Sheriff. We appreciate it. So long!"

The Sheriff hesitated. "Well, yes. I must get going. But let me ask this one question: Where do you hide your gold?"

"I don't have any gold, Sir. I'm just a plain old rock hound," laughed Franny.

The Sheriff left scratching his head. But finally, I thought, I knew the truth.

My dad came back early the next spring, and I got to wear my prom dress to the prom with Pete. Dad bought a big adobe house with three bedrooms and five acres. Dad tried to get Franny to move in with us and for a year she refused, but then Franny had a mild heart attack and was going to have open heart surgery. She asked if she could move in with us. Much to our surprise, Franny took us out to her backyard one day. In all of the five cracked toilets scattered around her back yard, were piles of silver ore.

"But Franny," I exploded, "You told us you didn't have anything left!"

"Well I told you I didn't have any gold. But I did have silver ore," she said as she scratched Percy under his chin.

"You and your dad can take this and sell it to Ron down at Tucson Metals. He will give you a check to pay the extra costs of the surgery," she said as she looked around the yard. "This place is getting to be too much, so when I get moved in to your place, let's sell this place and send Jennifer to college. My mining days are over."

And that is the tale of Gold Flower Road.

Just off the Yetman Trail

We just came off the Yetman Trail as it swoops around the edge of a large ridge called "Butch Cut." It is a dangerous hike with man-sized boulders at a couple of places that you must climb up. Two feet on the ground is a two-point hike. Three point is feet and stick or sticks. Five point is your butt. This is a five-point climb for me. The back of all my hiking pants are all worn out.

We hiked back to Sarasota Trailhead and stopped at Tucson Estates to get stamps at the post office. The original post office at "Cactus Cards" was shut down and they moved it to the "White's Ace Hardware Store." That how things roll in the twenty-first century Wild West, these days.

I joined the line forming towards the counter. There were strange young men with ten Amazon-taped packages, little old ladies with birthday presents for their grandchildren, and men with fistfuls of post cards all saying "Wish you were here."

A big, tall fellow with a full beard and a camo jacket slowly turned and eyeballed me and my frayed hiking outfit; patched shirt, faded shorts, dusty boots, and a happy wide brimmed hat with a "Think Sun" button.

"I bet you've never carried a gun in your life," he snarled at me.

I'm used to it; the male superiority of the American backwoods wilderness men.

I looked at him evenly. "Of course I have and I know how to use one." Being an old schoolteacher I can tell a bully from across a schoolyard.

He turned toward the counter and everyone took a step forward. His neck flourished into a deep red. Then he turned around and faced me again. His hand was on his gun holster under his jacket. He took a deep breath. "So where is it?'

I looked at him very steady, with no emotion, "Where is what?"

He sneered. "Your gun."

"I don't need it in the Ace Hardware Post Office." I said as I looked at my fist of mail and wished I was not there.

The old lady in back of me shifted nervously from side to side. The guy in front of me kept staring at me. "Where you from?" Everyone in this little tourist town was from somewhere else.

"I am from Oregon."

His brown eyes got a little soft-looking as he said "Bundy was there last year."

"Yep. I know all about him in Central Oregon and his Dad in Nevada." Unfortunately I know because it had been all over the news in Portland Oregon for months.

"Next!" yelled the Post Office counter person. The gun carry guy stepped up and bought his stamps and stomped off without a word.

"Boy you are lucky." Said the lady behind me. "He has reduced many a little old lady to tears."

I smiled. "Luck has nothing to do with it. It's all about charm." I said that with straight, dusty face in my ratty and patched hiking pants.

He-Who-Sits

He-Who-Sits in the morning.

He-Who-Sits-On-The-Mountain waits.
He watches the horsetail clouds fly.

(Weather's gonna change.)

He sees the bat doing loop-de-loops for insects.

(Bat's gonna bloat.)

He watches the sun-set skies.

(Sun's gonna burn up some day.)

Finally the sun sinks into the saw-toothed mountains.

(Where does it hide?)

He-Who-Sits-On-the-Mountain stays.
He looks at the forever-night skies.
He's been there ten thousand years.

He-Who-Sits in the evening

Gwenny Ruth

Delano St. Tucson, AZ

"She's gonna get cha! She's gonna get cha!" yelled Bobby, as he chased Billy around the kitchen table. "Gwenny Ruth is gonna get out of the nut house and she is gonna get you first, Billy!"

"No, Bobby, NO!" yelled Billy. He ducked under the table. His legs were quivering with fear. The boys just heard it on the radio news: Gwenny Ruth, the notorious female murderer of Arizona was getting out of the looney bin in California.

"She's gonna stab you first!" Bobby yelled as he poked Billy with the end of the broom.

"Eeeeek!" screamed Billy.

Mother stepped into the room. "Boys, take that catfight outside," she drawled in her best Okie voice.

"He started it Ma," cried Billy.

"I don't have a dog in this fight, Billy," said Mother as she carried a basket of wet clothes out to the yard.

Billy crawled to the other side of the table and darted out the screen door. Before the door could slam Bobby was out the door too. Intense waves of heat hit him and he slowed to a walk.

Billy was already feverously climbing the ladder to the roof of the shed and he sat on the adobe ledge. As soon as Bobby got there, Billy said "Tell me the story of Gwenny Ruth again."

"Oh, ok," sighed Bobby, although he was glad to do it again. It was their ritual to tell the story and act it out on the rooftop. Gwenny Ruth was one of their favorites.

First, Bobby would be the radio announcer: "Today, we have uncovered the strange story about Gwenny Ruth Judd, who was taken to the jail after the disappearance of a man. Police could not prove she killed anyone so she was let out on bail."

Billy chimed in. "So, Sheriff, I am a neighbor and I am smelling some strange smells coming out of Gwenny Ruth's house."

Bobby stood up. He was now the sherriff. "Wal, there is nothing we can do about that, just because Gwenny's house smells like dead cat."

"But it ain't no dead cat, sir," said Billy, playing his role.

"But, Gwenny Ruth stuffed a dead man in her trunk and took off on the train for California," continued Bobby.

Forgetting his role, Billy spoke up. "Didn't anybody smell the trunk?"

"This just in!" said Bobby as the announcer, "Gwenny Ruth has been tried and is sentenced to ten years in jail!"

"But Bobby, how did Gwenny get in the nut house?" asked Billy.

A long time ago, the boys asked Pa about Gwenny Ruth.

"Wal, boys," he said in his best Oklahoman authoritarian voice. "She is a woman of ill-repute, ya know what I mean?"

The boys didn't have a clue, but they nodded yes.

Pa continued: "They don't think anything will help that poor Ol' woman. You see, she left the town with a trunk. By the time she got off the train in San Francisco, that trunk was a'leak'en and a'stink'en."

"Leaking what?" asked Bobby.

"Blood." Said Pa. "That's when they sent her to jail and finally she got off for good behavior and they put her in the nut house."

"Now she can leave the nut house any time she wants to," said Bobby gravely as he sat on the ledge of the roof. "I bet anything she is going to pack a suitcase and come back to Tucson. When she does, she's gonna get you good, Billy! Maybe even pack you in a suitcase."

Billy burst out crying. "Why me?"

Bobby laughed. "I'll tell you what: if I can catch you at the kitchen door, she will get you. If not, then you are going to be safe. Get ready, set go!"

Billy ran across the roof and tripped. He flew off the roof and onto a lean-to three feet below. His hand punched through the roof and there was a snap. By then, Bobby was halfway down the ladder. "Root hog or die!" screamed Bobby.

Panicked, Billy pulled his arm out of the roof. A pain shot through his arm. He leapt off of the lean-to to the ground, stumbling a bit, but made it to the kitchen door.

Suddenly, an old green, hunch-back Chevy rolled into the driveway. "Hey, boys!" yelled Pa as he slammed the car door. "What are ya doen'? Play'en Cowboys and Indians?"

Bobby came sprinting up with Billy limping right behind with his arm dangling from his shoulder.

"We're playing Gwenny Ruth," said Bobby.

"What happened to you, sport? What's wrong with your arm?" asked Pa.

"Oh noth'in," said Billy with tears in his eyes.

"So, what did you say, Bobby?" said Pa.

"Gwenny Ruth. That crazy old lady," said Bobby.

Pa laughed. "Well you're say'en her name wrong, Bobby. She's not Gwenny. She's Winnie. That's Winnie Ruth Judd, the Trunk Murderer. Did she get out of the nut house again?"

Stairway to the Clouds

The Hugh Norris Trail

"So who the heck is this Hugh Norris?" asked Jan. Greg didn't hear her, so she kept babbling. "Is he some cowboy movie star or state senator?"

"Who?" said Greg. It was a bit windy and some unusual puffy clouds were swirling above the peaks.

Jan shook her head. "Hugh Norris. Who was he, a park ranger?"

"The hiking guide said he was a Tohono O'odham police chief," said Greg.

They walked to the iron ranger and signed the hiker's list. "This is going to be one scenic hike, Jan," smiled Greg, his eyes were gleaming.

They both tried to follow the trail with their eyes until it went out of sight, high among the steep ridges.

"Wow," they both said together.

These two had just taken up this hiking hobby and it was fun doing something together and sharing interesting moments. They looked forward to planning hikes during the work week and getting out whenever they could.

The Hugh Norris Trail was an outdoor stairway to the sky. Someone with a lot of energy had cut stone from some mine, hauled it somehow up the steep trail and literally built the stairway. It went straight up, then took a switchback, then climbed up even higher. The pair got a rhythm going as they marched along.

"You really have to lift your feet up high so you don't stub your feet," reflected Greg.

Jan started to laugh. "I'll say…ooof…there I go. I bet my toenails are going to be split!"

Higher and higher they plunged into the sky. Over the tops of two-hundred-year-old saguaros. High over the boulder-filled washes. Scanning the wide Arva Valley to the south and west. Peeking around the corner to see Picture Rocks Ridge from a strange new angle. There were buds on the saguaros and chollas and prickly pears were starting to flower their gem-like, gleaming flowers.

"It's like a stairway to the clouds," noted Jan as she quit counting stairs at about 342.

Greg shook his head. "I don't know how they got these heavy stones so far."

Soon they came to a saddle between peaks. They stopped and rested.

"Maybe they had a helicopter bring a load up here to the saddle. There were some wide corners where they could have off-loaded some of those stones too," said Jan.

The stairway continued on and around the next peak they watched a couple of buzzards circling the rocks for their lunch. Jan and Greg had lunch too around the next hillock. There, they could see the entire stretch of Picture Rocks Ridge in front of them. They were still climbing and finally the stairway stopped, but not the top of the rocky peaks.

Greg stopped again and washed down some water. "I'm sure glad I told Cousin Jimmy to pick us up at the King Canyon Trailhead by four o' clock."

Jan looked up. "Yeah we seem to still have a long way to go."

Now the trail got steep and there was a lot of rolling rock on the trail. The trail on the side hill was only a foot wide.

"Use your stick and take tiny steps from foot to foot!" yelled Greg, seeing that Jan was lagging behind. They took another switchback and found themselves going down another rolly-rock trail with a wall of granite on one side and eighty feet of air on the other.

First Greg slipped on the rock and then Jan did. When they got up, they really felt dizzy.

Meanwhile, Cousin Jimmy roared into the King Canyon parking lot at 4:05. He was relieved they were not waiting for him. He sat in the truck and listened to all of the NPR news.

Jan had fallen again and was really getting dizzy. Greg walked slowly and decided to let Jan go first so he could help her. They got to the top of the next peak on a corner and could not bear to look down. They looked up and saw another half mile of trail above them.

"Oh man," sighed Jan. "What happened to all those great stairs?"

"The ones you were complaining about?" said Greg, grumpily.

Later, it was almost 6:30 and the sun was setting. It was that time in the day when the horizon looked pink, blending into blue. Jimmy got out of the truck and went to the trail head and looked up it. He saw a line of five javelinas going down into the wash. No more hikers. No more cars in the parking lot, except his own. He tried calling Greg on his cell. No bars. Jimmy walked back to the truck and dozed off to sleep.

It was getting dark on the trail, but Greg said there should be more sun when they got on the east side. They could barely see the tops of all the peaks that they had climbed. They had to be almost on top of the last one. Only one steep hillside and they should be at the saddle. Jan was taking little steps when her foot slid off the side of the trail and she plunged over the side. Greg grabbed her leg and the end of her stick.

Meanwhile, back at the parking lot, Jimmy woke up to crunching in the gravel.

"Hey, buddy, you okay?" asked a deep voice.

Jimmy jumped and wondered for a moment where he was. The window of the truck was open and he had been sleeping out of it. There was a wide face looking in his side window. It was a Pima County sheriff.

Jimmy sleepily drawled. "Uh, yeah, hey there. I'm waiting for my cousins to come off the trail."

"Sorta late for that, unless they are doing a star gazing hike. Then ya gotta get a permit," said the Sheriff.

"I was supposed to pick them up at 4:00 p.m.," said Jimmy, scratching his head and getting out of the truck. "I think they were going to hike the Hugh Norris."

"Well, I'm sure they didn't have a flashlight, so I'll go get some," said the Sheriff.

They walked about a quarter of a mile and Jimmy's hips were screaming. "I can't go any farther, sir. I've had hip surgery a year ago and I'm not up to this hike."

"Well, what is your cell number? I'll call you when I find them and you go back. And on your way, see if you can get ahold of your cousins."

"Good thing I caught you in time," said Greg as they trudged upward.

"Yeah," said Jan. "I thought I was a goner. I felt like I was flying. We need a stairway to the stars."

"I felt like I was flying too," said Greg. He leaned over and kissed Jan's face. "Yeah, where is our stairway to the stars?" He felt a little rubber-legged as he walked along.

"How much longer do you think we have to walk?" asked Jan.

"I don't know… not much farther." Greg could hardly feel his legs. They felt numb.

Jimmy's cell phone rang, waking him up. It took him a moment to realize he'd been asleep in his truck all night.

He coughed. "Uh yeah. Hello."

"Hi, Jim. Sargent Adams from Pima County Sheriff's office calling."

"Did you find them?" asked Jimmy, as he looked at the clock on the dash. It was 2:00 a.m. in the still-dark morning.

"No. I didn't find them or any sign of them and now I'm over at the other end of the trail. They signed in yesterday at the iron ranger before they took off.

Where are you now?"

"I'm still at the parking lot. You hiked the entire trail" said Jimmy.

"Yes I did. Nice full moon at ten o'clock. Well, since you are still around, could you do me a favor, and come and get me in the park on Hohokam Road? I'm at the Hugh Norris trailhead. There are signs to find it. I am calling Search and Rescue right now," said the Sheriff.

The hikers trudged along. Greg laughed. "This is crazy, Jan. We must have gotten off on another trail or something in the dark. It just seems like we are walking forever. Jan? Jan?"

He turned to look at her. She looked like she was floating above the trail. Dreamily, she said "It is the stairway on the clouds. A stairway to the stars. How much higher will we go?"

After picking up the Sergeant Adams, and delivering him back to the squad car, Jimmy went home. He could barely see straight as he drove over Gates Pass. He collapsed on his couch and turned on the TV at his house. He was very sick to his stomach. He fell asleep.

The next day, he went out to the Hugh Norris Trailhead again and looked around, but he was not in shape to climb the mountain. He talked to some of the search and rescue people who were looking at footprints. Then he went home. How could Greg and Jan disappear like that?

By the end of the day, he saw it on TV:

"Breaking News: This just in—the missing hikers who have been gone for forty-eight hours have been found late this afternoon one-hundred feet below the Hugh Norris Trail in a boulder canyon. The Pima County deputy who lead the search and rescue team stated, 'It looked like they just fell from the sky.'"

Jim's phone rang.

Juan Carlos Trail

Juan Carlos lived near Valenzuela Road. It was an old wagon road used by the U.S. Calvary forty to fifty years before Juan Carlos came to this area. His hacienda and corrals were on the high part of his land. Out back, the land slanted downhill and beyond that was a strange bowl of earth which was in grassland. No buffel grass, like we have today, but a very fine sort of grass.

While the rest of the ranches bought bricks of hay from California, Juan Carlos–harvested hay from his desert grassland. He hand-dug the weeds out of the rocky soil and tried to divert water into the bowl without flooding it. He harvested hanks of hay and tied them with bits of rope, twisted brush, yarn, or even hay, itself. He would bring his donkey back to the paddock, all bristly with the hanks of hay tied with brilliant colors. The trail goes to the field, but goes no farther. The field is still there, along with the old adobe house and the paddocks built with old mesquite wood and live, bristly Ocotillo stalks.

Buffalo Soldier

I stand on this berm, overlooking a wash.
Rock cliffs hold desert bristling—it is so lush.
The desert inhales, there's a wind and a rush.
Apache are weaving their way through the brush.

"Why go there?" they said, "You are single and free!"
"I owe this." I said. I joined the cavalry.
A horn tooted Charge! As I dropped to my knee.
Indians spilled o'er the cliffs as I shot three.

We were young, brave, and happy once in our new life,
I had a homestead, six horses—loving wife.
Then when I came home it was burned down—no life.
The only thing left was a long-bladed knife.

So o'er these mountains and canyons I roam.
Every new fire ring, my hearth and my home.
From Mexican border to desert high loam.
In the Canyons of Warsaw—hills of hard stone.

(Someday I'll be buried, so sad and alone,)
(In the Canyons of Warsaw—hills of hard stone.)

Your Broad Face

Your broad face
Is like a blank canvas
Etched with lines of emotion.

From picture-perfect perfection
to washed, shiny, and solemn.
A grimace here, a sneer there,
Eyes aroused or astonished.

Glamourous or plain,
No matter what the mask may be,
There is always a smile to cover the pain.
I love…your broad face.

The Naturalist Hiker

(An Essay)

On the Utah/Arizona Border

Like Rocks

A chemistry experiment in slow-motion suspension: that is our story of the earth. Like rocks; ever changing. How it is now, where it came from, and where it is going. It may remain a mystery and yet I strive to understand it. Here is an example of a hike after a rainstorm.

Bright flashes burst our eyes open in the middle of the night. And explosion of sound a few beats later. A gully-washing thunder storm blew upon our camp the other day. The red rock surrounding us was beaten by the harsh rain. The rocks turned dark—such a dark red that that they blushed by the light of day. When they could absorb no more in its dusty cracks, they wept, spilling over, sending rivulets, shooting water falls over the rounded lips of boulders. The cliffs and the vegetation were all crying with an echoing drip, drip, drip to the ground.

Mother Nature gently applied the desert varnish to the rocks. The chemical reaction darkened, and enhanced the painted, rippling outlines. Just add some soft H_2O and sit back and watch the chemical reaction.

Later, a sun break flashed upon the high buttes, followed by a light show of spotlighted features all over the region. The gooey red clay mud formed fast back into a firm floor of the desert as we sat and watched the natural pageant. We waited before jumping onto the trail right away because we knew that some clay spots will be soaked and our boots will make ugly marks on the land digging in ruts in the trail and uprooting the natural composition of the land.

The Magic Stones

Soon, the ruddy earth was hardened like a tile. After coffee and oatmeal, we headed out on the trail. We followed the footprints of dinosaurs and ancient people caught in a similar rainstorm as they danced in a small lake or stream. Today, the stream banks are hoisted high and the hiker climbs up the ridges to see the ancient marks. A herd of three-toed "dinos" dancing across the rocks. Hikers can follow the imprinted stream rocks lying across the ridge. They are scattered about like rock ice flows.

The landscape is so vast and the next thing we see is an entire ancient village hiding on top of another ridge in plain sight! Of course it is on the highest ridge around for protection. The ancient village looms over a wide, flat floodplain which we know from history was their farm grounds with some simple irrigation. We circled the perimeter of the village, looking at the strange rock work. Some of it is sitting upright rather than flat. There were small doors and windows which were used as listening portals from the other rooms, and mysterious food storage circles.

This high ridge is long and slashes across a huge area. The park rangers call this type of hill a "reef." Sprinkled on this naturally red pavement, I found many strange and pretty green rocks. The way they were arranged across the macadam looked very pleasing to the eye, as if some artistic park ranger had set up this artistic display at the crack of dawn. But I know this was far from the case because a park ranger is hard to find in the wilderness these days. They are most likely hiding in their offices hoping they will not be laid off.

I plucked a few of the green rocks and put them in my pocket for further analysis and I looked over the mountain horizon for a clue as to where the green rock came from. Above the red rock towers loomed a tip of a peak of what someone called "The Silver Ridge." Those old explorers must have been colorblind, because they looked green to me.

After our hike of reefs and ridges, I pulled my green rocks out of my pocket. They were not as bright in hue as they had been on the trail. That seemed natural since the rain had brightened them up. Hours later these beautiful rocks were yellow, sort of a dull tan yellow and not very interesting. I put the rocks under the drip-line of our camp ramada to see if the rock would brighten up. No such luck. I am still seeking an explanation about these magic stones.

Hike up Aravaipa Canyon

Opening the canyon he lets us come in.
The creek canyon opens our trail much wider.
Cottonwoods mark where we have just once been.
I want to hike this with Gary Snyder.

Birds chant their songs from each side of the stream.
Feet flowing in water, it's part of our dream.
The cliffs growing higher the shade goes to dawn.
I follow Gary in silence, along.

The stream gets narrow, cliffs shelter our throng.
We hike with sticks, which steady us along.
We twist and we turn and at noon we turn back.
The sun shines high in its celestial crack.

We now are amazed at what we've not seen.
A vision below on a stage much wider.
The hawks and buzzards high up on a breeze.
I took this hike with my friend, Gary Snyder.

The Bar at the End of the Trail...

The Dutchman Trail
On Superstition Mountain

"Come on," said Robert impatiently as he grabbed my arm and helped to hoist me up over some large boulders, graveled with slippery, gravel.

I was exhausted. My boots slipped over the rocks. I was barely able to keep standing. We had been hiking the

Dutchman Trail for two nights—two sleeps, as the Native Americans say. The first day was fun and the second day was full of high assaults and beautiful county. This was the third day and we were supposed to camp at the State Park and be home tomorrow.

After slipping, sliding and crawling off the boulders, I sat by the trail of firm ground and drank the last of my water bottle, huffing and puffing from the exertion. "I just don't know if I can go on, Robert."

He laughed. "Of course you can. One more ridge and we will be going downhill and at the end of the trail, there is a big old-fashioned Western saloon."

"Really?" I said, amazed.

"Yeah. One ridge, downhill, time for an IPA!" He chanted it again and again as he got me up on my feet.

On and on we hiked. The switchbacks looped us up around a huge ridge.

The hairpin curve was spectacular with a small waterfall of splashing down and under the trail in a little wooden culvert.

"The Dutchman put that in there so the trail would not wash away. It was the last landmark he could remember before the lost mine." Said Robert. He paused long enough for me to wash my face and hands to revive myself. We filled our water bottles with the fresh, cold and clear liquid. But when we started back up on the trail, Robert was walking twice as fast. I could not keep up with him.

Finally on another sharp curve, we reached the end of the ridge. Robert was waiting for me at the look-out point. The view was spectacular. I had just enough time to snap a few pictures and realized that my partner had taken off down a steep incline with no end in sight. Down, down, down we went zigzagging the switchbacks, never seeing the bottom. After a while, my shins were aching. Still, we went on.

The sun was pretty low in the sky when we left the ridge and now we were in deep shade. Sometimes I thought Robert was running. I tried to do the same with a bit of a jog, but after a while I stumbled and my legs went to jelly. I sat in a heap.

A voice called below me. "Jerri! Where are you? Jerri? Jerri?" I looked down and there was Robert, two levels below me. I just sat there.

"I'm here. I'm here." I gasped.

I could see Robert moving back up the trail. When he moved up one switchback, I mustered all my strength, still gasping for air. I felt like a three-legged person, with my hiking stick, trying to get up and start walking.

Robert looked up and smiled. "That's my girl! Only a mile and a half mile to go."

Luckily, we were soon off of the winding trail and onto a wide wash. There to one side of the wide graveled desert was a ramshackle building. We had made it to the bar at the end of the trail and it was nightfall.

Inside, the saloon was even more gloomy than the dark night. Over the bar was a golden light, covered with dust and cobwebs and a row of antelope of various sizes, shocked into silence by a shot long ago. There was a man behind the bar with messy red hair. "What'll you folks have?" He smiled a gap-toothed grin.

Robert shouted over some loud twangy music. "We'd like two IPAs."

The barkeep looked us up and down. "IPA.... IPA... I still don't know what that means. I have some Day-chutes in a bottle."

"Great! "We will take two." Yelled Robert. The guy brought us two a-piece. Robert does not like to sit at the bar when it is crowded, with his back to everyone, so he wandered around with his two beers and his backpack. He landed in a booth towards the back.

Some extremely filthy guy came out of the bathroom and Robert caught his eye. "Hi there, do you have the time?"

The guy's eyes gleamed. "I've got time to waste but no time piece. Hawk has my watch." His shoulders slumped as he was recalling a bad time.

Robert took a swig of his beer. "So where's this Hawk?"

"He's over at the card table," said the filthy guy.

Robert got up and talked to a couple of guys at the card table. They talked him into playing cards. He talked them into playing for matchsticks as he pretty much used up all his money on beer.

The night got longer and longer. They kept playing cards. I drank both my beers and fell asleep in the booth.

The next thing I know, the sun is shining through a hole in a tent. I could hear Robert rummaging around outside, breaking sticks to start a fire. He was wildly thrashing around and I stuck my head out of the tent. We were still up in the mountains, somewhere. I was so tired, I could hardly think.

"What the heck?" he murmured. He looked at me. "Where the heck are all my matches?" he yelled.

Iron Ranger Song at Picket-Post Trail

We salute the Iron Ranger
Marching merrily along.
The trail guides us to a place
Which we have never known.

With our boots, pack, and trekking stick,
As we power up the rise,

The scene below and all around
Is amazing to our eyes.

He nods to trail and lends a hand.
Our Iron Ranger salutes our band.
Leaning up the trail head, rusty,
We leave our guide for the trail, so dusty.

So long before our hikers rule,
The miners came with packs and mule.
They drove them up the switchback trail
Stuffed with food, some tools, and mail.

Then down they came from the mountain mine
Loaded with ore, one mule at a time.
The iron ranger and picket-post.
Stand today as a test of most.

Chorus:

At trail head,
The hiker's wend
One by one,
To trail's end

The steep terrain
The hiker's pain.
Up zig and zag
Submit to gain.

The Bar at the End of the Trail

Part 2

Luckily, I had some matches in my backpack. I thought about teasing Robert about losing all his matches in the card game, but finally decided, after a cup of coffee, that I should not say anything. I was told that I was so dehydrated that we did not make it to the end of the trail. I did not want Robert to think I was a looney; we had only been friends for about six months.

I felt rejuvenated after my night, but I noticed that Robert was a little surly. We were a day late, so we would not be staying in the State Park and Robert would have to call his friend to pick us up at the end of the Dutchman Trail.

Since I had already been on the trail in my dreams, I could predict every land mark along the way. That seemed really eerie, but at the same time, it made the hike feel shorter.

When we got to Dutchman Creek where the wooden water culvert was, I expected Robert to tell me the story, but instead, he filled up on water and kept going. I stayed for a bit, washing my hands and face and filling up my water bottle.

It was such a nice place, that I didn't want to leave it. I looked up to see two men coming up the trail. They were very dark and silent. They looked like the Apache natives I had seen in history books. They acted like I was invisible. One man was carrying a little baby and the other had a little two-year-old in tow. They were wearing layers of clothing; a suit jacket, a vest, a white cotton shirt with a ragged bottom, an apron-like shift of the same cloth and white leggings wrapped around their legs. One had boots the other had leather moccasins. They went to work gathering water in some sort of animal bladders, bending over skillfully, the one man holding the baby in a sling the whole time. The little girl broke away from the man and looked at me crouched by the trail wall. She was barefoot and had a small woven shawl over her shoulders and her cotton dress. She walked up to me and held out her hand. I did the same. She put her fist on top of mine and deposited something hard in my hand. She turned and stepped back to the man.

I looked down at the hard thing in my hand. It was a creamy sea shell. Shells come from the beach, such a long, long way from this sky island desert mountain.

When I looked back up, all four people were gone. I panicked, grabbed all my things and rushed to catch up with Robert. "Did you see those Indians?" I said breathlessly.

He frowned. "No. What Indians?

I told him what happened. Robert tried to humor me: "Well they may have been resting from going up the mountain and got off the trail before I came down. Then they got back on the trail....Could be part of a re-enactment of the Apache Trail Days."

That was good of him, but I could tell he was wondering about my brain and the dehydration and exhaustion from the day before. We finally made it to the sandy wash, marking the end of the trail. There was the building, just as I remembered it. I ran to the front of the place and saw that the roof was caved in! There was a sign that said "Closed."

Robert laughed. "No one has had a drink in that bar since Statehood."

"Wait! You said we were going to come down here and have an IPA." I exclaimed.

"It's an old joke. The guys told me that story too the last time I hiked this trail. I thought I was going to have a cold one too and I kept going. The thought of that got you down off the mountain, didn't it?" He looked at me with love.

As Robert called his friend to pick us up at the old bar, I felt in my pocket and took out the sea shell the little Apache girl had given me.

Hiking Terms

Ammo Boxes—These metal boxes can be found in rocky piles (cairns) on mountain peaks and ridges. Hikers put them there with a pencil and notebook for people to sign in with names and dates. Over the years, it makes interesting reading for hikers who have "made it."

BLM—Bureau of Land Management. Federal Program which manages grasslands, deserts, mines, and rangelands.

Bushwacking—Going off of the recommended trail. NOT a good idea! There are many ways to cause erosion on hillsides or ruin the patina of the desert sands and soils. You will find yourself getting injured easily by doing this or worse! You could get very lost! Do this only in the case of emergency. I always feel more confident on an established trail.

Cairn—A stack of stones to indicate the trail. Used where a path cannot be seen such as in rocky terrain. Stacks of stones with something inside of on top of mountains.

Dispersed Camping—A primitive fire ring and camp spot. No facilities such as water or latrine. On range land, wilderness, or desert land, mostly BLM.

Fall Line—The straight talus or wash down the slope of a mountain. Driven by gravity or water. Do not hike these lines. You cannot build a trail on them.

Forest Service Roads—Numbered roads on stakes, (sometimes with corresponding maps) Wildlife Refuges and National and State Parks also have these roads.

Iron Ranger—A post with a sign (the old ones were made with iron poles) some with a book to sign in before you take a hike and after to sign out. Sometimes there are maps available, but these days, maps and sign in books are (sadly) rare.

Lookie—A short trail to a view point or a viewpoint itself, just off the main trail.

Loop Trail—Takes you out and brings you back. Possibly a more interesting trail. Usually a longer one.

Out and Back Trail—Just what it says, which can be nice if you only use it a few times. Sometimes I turn and look in back of me to see what I am missing the other way.

Ridge—The top spine of a hill or mountain. In some rocky locations, there are also Long, rocky mounds of loose rock formations called **reefs.** You see or climb these in places like Utah.

Ramada—A shade structure in a camp. The southwest Natives build them out of juniper (or other types of wood) posts. The shade on top of the frame is ocotillo a spikey, woody plant. State parks usually provide a shade structure made out of modern materials.

Saddle—A low ridge between two higher peaks.

Service Road—Roads reserved for Forest Service, BLM, National Park, or State Park workers only. They are used for maintenance and forest fires.

Sky Islands—The high mountain groups that loom three-thousand to nine-thousand feet above the desert floor.

Switchback—An S or Z shape trail going up a steep incline of a mountain or hill.

Two-track—Usually an old jeep road that is now being used as a hiking trail. Jeep Roads were popular after World War II when the troops came back to Arizona. Veterans tried their luck at mining for a while, without much success.

Trailhead—The start of a trail, sometimes with a small parking lot. Usually they have names or numbers. Sometimes they lead to larger trails like the Arizona Trail or Pacific Crest Trail.

Wash—A dry waterway such as a creek or river. Wash walking is hard work, especially going "up-water." However on a windy, gusty day, it keeps you out of the wind. Many interesting plants and animals are found in washes.

Water Bar—High line of rocks, railroad ties, or steps to divert water from Washing out the trail.

Virga—A weather condition, common in the desert. It is ephemeral rain that evaporates before it touches the ground.

Virga

Rain that never touches the ground.
Dew point above which flies through the air.
It kisses the mountains. The winds do sound.
But like all rain, it is blind
To the world all around.

Lightning Source UK Ltd.
Milton Keynes UK
UKHW041200140620
364910UK00006BA/1032